UNCLE BOB BUILDS A BOAT

MARK W JARVIS WITH CHRIS POWELL

Mark W Jarvis
with
Chris Powell

ISBN: 1527206386

ISBN-13: 978-1527206380

DEDICATION

To all those who recognize themselves in this book. It is not about you, but we might have borrowed a little of your essence. With everlasting gratitude to our "Karries" - without your love we would be lesser people.

Prep-production copy.

"If you want to build a ship, don't drum up people to collect wood and don't assign them tasks and work, but rather teach them to long for the endless immensity of the sea".

Antoine de Saint-Exupery

CONTENTS

ACKNOWLEDGMENTS

There are many without whom this book would never have been written. It was inspired by people who Chris and I have known and worked with, admired and feared, but most of all learnt from over the years. You are too many to name, but particular thanks needs to go to my daughters who indulged my passion for sailing long enough to become much better at it than I will ever be. They encouraged me to put down on paper some thoughts and then took time to read and edit. Chris Powell, who also warrants special mention, not only got me to actually finish the text but managed to remain a good friend throughout the process. Finally Luther Spicer who provided the illustrations that capture something that words cannot express.

Thank you

1

UNCLE BOB BUILDS A BOAT

"Evening. They tell me you want to build a boat."

I hadn't said a word to him... Villages!

I didn't intend to build a boat when we moved to the coast. I didn't even really have sailing in my mind. I had a romantic memory of the village from past holidays so when the chance came to buy the local accountancy firm it sounded perfect. We had both worked hard for a long time. We liked the city, we knew what we were doing, we liked the friends who did jobs like ours, the technology, the hustle and bustle and I was sure it was where I belonged. It was – well it was one of those spur of the moment, 'if we don't do it now we never will' decisions. Four weeks later the flat was sold, everything we owned was in boxes and we were sitting eating chips on the beach wondering what we had done. Still, our friends were only two hours, away by train and they were bound to come and visit us at weekends. No one in the village spoke to us. They certainly didn't understand me in the office and now even the guy I was offering to spend large amounts of money with was treating me like a child, not a customer – these villagers needed to go on some courses.

I sat on the bench and sipped my beer, trying to play it cool.

We exchanged pleasantries about the weather, the standard of the beer and village life for about ten minutes. Then he said, "Come and see me at 9.00 am tomorrow at the yard and bring your boots."

I walked home up the hill. Nothing had been said and nothing was really any further forward and now he wanted me to bring boots to a further meeting. Frankly I had no idea how these people made money.

Karri knew something was up as soon as I walked in the door. We chatted about the experience and tried to make some sense of what had happened. It wasn't logical, but Karri knew this was the right thing to do and for her, just then, that was what mattered.

I had no idea where my sailing boots were. I had packed them away in a box at least two moves ago and really they could have been anywhere. Karri did her best to be supportive and encouraging, but I was flailing around rummaging through box after random old box, justifying to anyone who was listening why it might be that the boots would be in a box with vinyl records or university course notes or my parents' dinner service! Finally, they were found in a box of old sports kit along with a squash racket (I don't remember the string breaking) and a tracksuit top that I wasn't sure had ever fitted me.

So I left the house just in time with a kiss from Karri and frustration with village life in my heart.

2

LET'S GO FOR A WALK

I strode down the hill. I tried to remember what it was that had got me to this point. Having moved to the village and unpacked the boxes, Karri and I had made the most of the late summer. We would wander down the hill to the harbour most evenings. When the weather got too bad we would sit in the bus shelter. We were trying to do our bit to be part of the village – being seen about and so on. I was starting to meet one or two of the locals through my work but they seemed reluctant to chat much or tell me really anything more than I needed in relation to my work for them. The only one who initiated anything was Graeme.

He invited Karri and I to the sailing club prize giving.

We sat people-watching all evening. There were all sorts there. But the most memorable thing of the evening was seeing the mid-week trophy being presented to Graeme. It was beautiful. I was a little bit worse for wear and somewhere in it all I think I promised to win the trophy one day. This seemed to cause much amusement amongst the locals. I remember one particularly confident member stridently telling me that the trophy couldn't be won by anyone from outside the village.

"It's not rocket science," I said to Karri the next morning. "Just how hard can it be? Build a boat, learn to race and win the trophy – easy. It's not as though this lot are Olympic champions or anything."

There was the small matter of finding the money and someone to build the boat. I was up for doing most things, but I knew I was unlikely to win the prize quickly if I started out by building the boat myself. Besides which, the local economy could do with the help and I was sure I could improve things round here if they could only see the benefits of some of the things I had learnt in years of working for some of the top companies in the world.

The bittersweet news of my great aunt's death just after Christmas was the final tipping point to finding a boat builder. She had left me a gift in her will 'to be spent on something fun for you and your family'. Well, in my mind she might as well have said to go and build a boat and win the race series – strangely, Karri didn't see it quite as clearly but agreed to me asking around in the village for a boat builder.

Work seemed like the obvious place to start and sure enough there was immediate consensus about the person I should talk to, although a slight raising of eyebrows about my master plan. Uncle Bob was the man apparently. He ran the yard on the far side of the harbour, had been building boats for many years – most of the ones that raced locally were built by him. The suggestion was that I should go to the pub at 5.00 that evening because he nearly always had a pint on the way home. I was keen to go over to the yard there and then, but the locals were adamant this was not the best plan and so I returned to my work and waited, watching the clock grind slowly round till 4.45 pm.

I went to the bar and ordered a pint and enquired who Uncle Bob was. He was sitting outside on a bench with his dog lying at his feet watching what was left of the daylight, sipping his pint and greeting those who passed. I recognised him. He was part of the sailing boys' group occasionally and had definitely been at the prize giving but didn't win anything (or not that I remembered). So it was that I was now trudging down the hill in an old pair of sailing wellies to talk to a local with no customer skills about building a boat.

Was I mad?

I arrived at the boat sheds just before 9.00 am. There were four sheds of different sizes. It was hard to work out which was the reception or main shed.

Don't these people understand signs?

I wandered round the yard looking up at the boats in cradles on the hard standing and trying to figure out which door to try first. As I stood looking, I felt a warm presence by my right leg. I looked down and saw a dog. He was a difficult dog to define. He clearly had working dog heritage and was big enough to have a shoulder that brushed above my knee, but beyond that he was a bit of a mixture. However, there was something pure, honest and trustworthy about him and as he walked ahead of me it seemed to make sense to follow him. He walked to a small door in the second shed and so I went over and opened it. I followed him in and within five strides I was standing next to the guy from the previous night. Looked like I had stumbled on the right place.

"Good to see you," he said. "Did you bring your boots?"

"Yes," I replied.

"Well let's go for a walk then. Come on, Dirk."

With that he turned and headed for the door and Dirk, now with an enthusiastic bounce to his stride, followed him. I dutifully followed a few paces behind, not really knowing why or what was going to happen next.

What did happen next was that we walked for over an hour along muddy winter lanes up the hill behind the village and into the woods to come out at the cliff top overlooking the next bay. As we walked Uncle Bob asked me about all sorts of things – why I had moved to the village, how Karri and I had met, the job I had in the city, where my parents lived, holidays... It seemed we spoke about everything other than building a boat.

I found this frustrating. I was a busy man, I had a business of my own to run and I had no idea what time this was all going to be over. But as we walked and talked I warmed to Uncle Bob. He was genuinely interested in me and Karri.

By the end of the walk I was sure he knew more about us than anyone else in the village. As we came out of the wood on the way back down the lane to the boat yard he asked if there was anything I needed to know about the yard.

"What do you city types call it – supplier evaluation?"

I was stumped – I knew nothing about his yard but couldn't think of anything worthwhile to ask.

We meandered our way into the shed. He offered me a cup of tea and we sat down at a table.

"What does success look like?" Uncle Bob asked me.

Without thinking I said, "Holding the mid-week race series trophy."

"Good," was his response. "I can work to that."

We chatted a little more as we drank tea and then I realised I need to get back to work. As we left, Uncle Bob said, "Are you free next Wednesday at 4.00 pm if I get the team together to meet you?"

"Yes – I think so."

"OK, well let me know when you get back to the office. Over the next week can you chat to Karri and the rest of your family about what success looks like for you and write it down? We have your definition but I think the others may have a different view."

Still nothing. Three hours of tramping through mud and so far all he knew was I wanted to win a trophy. What kind of spec was that? He clearly needed an introduction to a project management course and some of the other locals needed to think a bit harder about who they recommended to me. This sort of approach wouldn't win any work in the city. No detail, no scope, no cost... maybe I could help him.

3

WHAT DOES SUCCESS LOOK LIKE?

Who would have thought that I could spend so much time talking to people about what success looked like in relation to a boat? Even Mum had an opinion and I thought she hated boats! Karri was keen for me to follow my dream but saw the whole thing from a more family-focussed perspective; teaching the kids to sail, having my Dad down for weekends and taking friends round to the next bay for picnics.

Dad sent one of his lists – it arrived in the post. No covering letter or anything, just a bulleted list:

Total cost not to exceed £100k

- A boat that meets and exceeds current CE floatation and righting criteria.
- A boat that can be towed to other ports.
- A fast boat that wins races.
- A safe boat to cross The Channel in.
- An easy boat to sail.
- An easy boat to clean and maintain.

I started to doodle ideas on the end of the list as I looked out of the office window.

- A beautiful boat that friends admire.
- A place to take friends.
- A boat to teach my children to sail on.
- A boat my Dad can sleep on when he comes to stay.

Oh dear, the list was getting long and some of the things I wanted seemed to contradict each other. I needed help. It was time to talk to the experts. Paul – he was a consultant doing project management, he could help. I rang him.

"Really," he said. "they don't have a methodology! How do they make any money?"

"I am asking myself the same question."

"Well, I suggest you need a requirements capture session and then you need to prioritise your requirements. They'll need to be evaluated against a cost, time and quality matrix to give you a working specification."

"Thanks Paul – I knew it was worth talking to you. When are you coming down to see us?"

"Soon, mate, soon – just got a few things to sort out this end then we'll call. Say hi to Karri."

After two more days of struggling with everything I decided to go and see Uncle Bob again.

"Hello", he said. "Has it all got a bit complex?"

How did he know?

"Well, yes it has. You suggested talking to the rest of my family, which was a good idea. Some of the things they suggested are great but some of them have got me thinking and now I am nowhere near as clear as I was about the original description of success." I replied, as he was getting out a canvas bag. It didn't have much in it. We sat down at a table in the corner of the workshop and Uncle Bob calmly said "What was the original success you wanted?"

"To win the mid-week trophy."

"Has that changed?"

"No."

"So what's the problem?" He had a slight wry smile as he asked.

"Some of the other ideas don't fit with that, but they are good ideas."

"OK – let's hear the ideas."

I started to list them and Uncle Bob started to write them down on a big sheet of paper in front of me – he appeared to be putting them into different sections.

"Is that it?" he said, as I slowed to a halt. I checked through Dad's list and tried to remember all that Karri and Mum had said – oh, and Sally from the city – not sure why I even asked her but she had said I needed to think about re-sale value.

We sat for a moment looking at the list.

"So, let's chat about 'safe to cross The Channel in'. What does that look like to you?"

I started to talk, then stopped, went back, started again.

He asked a further question. I restated my first comment then thought more and altered it slightly. He kept probing and pushing and I kept trying to leap to a single all-embracing sentence that would be the answer. I could feel the sailors in the pub bar laughing at me. I knew so little about the boat I wanted I couldn't describe it and yet I was the man who said he would win the trophy. Finally he said, "It's OK to not have the answer and it is also OK to have to explain your answer. The important thing here is that we treat these success statements as flexible until we have bent them enough to be certain what the real shape is – then we can be certain that they're fit for purpose."

"But how can you build a boat if you don't know what I want?"

"True, I need to understand what you need but that is often more than the original vision – Henry Ford used to say 'If I asked my customers what they wanted they would say a faster horse!' The more I know about you, your family and your friends, the better the boat I will build for you. Your mate Paul is right though – it can't just be about you, so there will be things we have to have even though you may never use them. Some will meet legal requirements and some will be to help you sell her if you ever need to. I am not building a boat for now. This boat will probably outlast you and certainly me, so we must think about the long term. But I'll keep these to the minimum and make her as much your boat as I can – you need to feel at home in her. Happy sailors are fast sailors."

We then ran through the list together, putting the success statements in ESSENTIAL, IMPORTANT, NICE TO

HAVE, NOT REQUIRED. Once we had the list, Uncle Bob said "Good – I can work with that. Do you want to take it home and think about it more?"

I thought I had better sleep on it so arranged to deliver my final list the following day. Talking it through with Karri that evening over dinner it seemed that I had rehearsed and organised my thoughts well in my time with Uncle Bob and we only agreed minor changes to the list, moving something from Important to Nice to have.

4

THE TEAM - NO SURPRISES

When I dropped the list off to Uncle Bob later in the week he suggested we get the team together for an initial meeting. Uncle Bob got out a piece of paper with a wave shape on it and started to write names at various places. Mine and his names were already there, as was Eric's near the crest of the wave, with Mart underneath.

"I am not sure where to put Tim at the moment. I haven't seen him outside sailing," he said in a distracted way. "Jan will be needed." He wrote her name just before Eric and then said, "That leaves us needing someone who checks and controls - Rick... He is very busy and a bit last minute but he will challenge and question what we are doing."

The wave seemed full of names and Uncle Bob looked happy. I was confused but didn't like to ask – these villagers seemed to have some strange ways of doing things.

We discussed possible dates and times. It was surprisingly difficult to get six people in a room together for the first time. And so it was that two weeks later I left the office early, telling Jean that I would not be back until tomorrow, and returned to the boat yard, with some apprehension, to meet the team.

I knew that there were more sheds around the central hard standing but I had only ever been into the small one that Uncle Bob had been in on the first day. I met him there again but straight away he suggested we went over to a bigger shed opposite, where the rest of the team would be gathering.

In the corner of the big shed was what was called 'the office' – I knew this because it was written in chalk on the door; otherwise the wood blended with the walls of the shed and camouflaged the meeting room. When we opened the door the first thing I noticed was the wall of heat coming out like a tsunami against the cold of the shed.

"Come in quickly! We need to keep the heat in – Jan doesn't function if the temperature falls." I moved into the room and found four people already there.

"Have a seat everyone – who are we missing? Rick?" asked Uncle Bob.

Everyone laughed and almost as though that was his cue, the final person entered the room.

"We did say 10.00 am, didn't we?" he said, looking at his

watch and sorting himself out. He had clearly run from somewhere and was a little breathless. We all settled and looked to the end of the table where Uncle Bob was sitting.

"Morning, everyone! Thanks for coming on this cold day."

Uncle Bob introduced me and suggested that we went round the table and said a little bit about ourselves, said what our role on the boat build would be, what our sailing experience was and then one other thing that we all should know.

The person who had told me to come into the office quickly was the first to start.

"Morning, I'm Eric, master carpenter at this yard," (There was a slight ooh from the others at this description.) "Oh all right I am the chippie! I have been sailing around here for as long as I can remember. When we race together I'm the main sheet trimmer and general eyes of the boat. I feed information to the skipper about where the other boats are. The thing you need to know about me is that I don't work on Sunday. Me and the Mrs are involved in the local church and so I have to be there on a Sunday – it's important to us."

"Hello, I'm Jan. Uncle Bob has asked me to be the sail maker for this boat. I don't sail but I do have a Master's in aerofoil design and I think the results of my boats speak for themselves. The thing you need to know about me – I don't like the cold, hence I don't sail in this country, and I'll be at Cowes Week every year."

"Morning, my name is Mart. I'm the rigger for this boat. I sail here in the harbour most weeks, sometimes in my own boat but normally with Graeme – as I prefer being at the front of the fleet! I do foredeck work for Graeme. When

I'm not sailing you can normally find me in the pub with friends talking about sailing."

"Hi, I'm Tim. I'm the apprentice here. I have a development classes racing dinghy – I won the junior trophy last year but now I have to race with the adults." There was a pause while Tim thought. "My girlfriend is called Janice." There was a cheer from the rest of the table and Tim went red but smiled as Mart patted him on the back.

"Rick – morning everyone. I will be the electrician on this boat. I sail in the next bay with a team hoping to get into the top three in Cowes Week this year. The thing you need to know about me is I hate people being late!" There was much jeering at this and it took a moment or two for Uncle Bob to settle the room down.

Nodding towards me, Uncle Bob said, "And you...?" I introduced myself and my said a bit about my background in sailing and then announced I was an accountant. There were a few glances across the table at this.

"It's OK," said Uncle Bob. "He is perfectly normal, for an accountant!" With everyone now introduced and settled into a comfortable environment Uncle Bob moved on.

"So, we all know what we are doing here. Most of you have worked together. We haven't had a suitable boat for Rick for a few years but he does repairs for us so he knows his way around the yard. Tim is new to the team but I've known him for several years now and I know he will work hard and will listen to us as he's keen to learn the trade. As ever, the key thing for us all is that there are no surprises as we go through the build; mistakes and problems will come up, but these are only significant if they come as a surprise to someone else in the team – particularly me. No surprises."

5

THE PLAN

"I think it's time for you to tell us what you would like us to build for you." Uncle Bob catches my eye and gives me an encouraging smile.

"I suppose it starts with me sitting in a bus stop with my wife. We moved down here from the city when I got the chance to buy Neil's accountancy practice – you know the one at the top of Church Road. We were admiring the boats moored in the harbour. I then went to the prize giving – Graeme invited me – and I saw the mid-week trophy. It was love at first sight. That's when I decided I wanted to try and win the prize. No, not try – I *wanted* to win it! After a bit of batting it back and forth with Karri, my wife, I decided to find someone to build me a winning boat. Everyone pointed me to Uncle Bob, so I assumed he must be the best." I smiled back at Uncle Bob and the team enjoyed the little jest. "We've been talking about it since then and I think we have a set of success statements that will give you a clear idea of what success looks like to me." I was learning the language of working with Uncle Bob. The team looked pleased and waited for me to run things through with them. I got out the list that Uncle Bob and I had agreed and then began.

The team started asking questions, just like Uncle Bob had done. Mart was the most vocal. He pulled at the statements to make sure he really understood what was being asked of him. His favourite line seemed to be:

"Let me repeat that back to you... Is that correct?"

This time, however, I knew more about these statements and how we got there, so having rehearsed the discussion, with Uncle Bob and with Karri I was able to walk the team through my thinking with some confidence. During this discussion Uncle Bob said very little. He just sat there and watched the team. I later asked him why he hadn't said much and he replied, "You were doing such a great job on your own I didn't need to get involved." He did say that he was watching the team to make sure they all understood what was required and that they all were engaged with the build.

"If you lose them early it can be ages before you get them on board properly and these foundational meetings are vital. You'd be surprised how often I have seen people get four or six weeks into a build and suddenly say, 'Why are we doing it like this?' Just shows they have not listened in the early meeting."

Once the questions had died down Uncle Bob got out a large sheet of paper on which was a very basic outline of a boat. He described some dimensions and explained his reasons.

He then said, "OK we know each other well enough to know everyone here will do a good job in their own area. What we need to focus on now are the main areas that affect us all. Shall we start with the mast?"

Suddenly there was a great amount of interest from all around the table. It was clear the mast involved them all and the way the mast was made was going to have an impact on all sorts of things I had never thought of. Everyone chipped in with opinions, comments and suggestions. However, it was hard to see where the solution was going to come from. Next up was the location and type of motor. I was surprised Jan had an opinion about this, but apparently it would alter the balance of the boat and therefore the sail plan. During this discussion Jan seemed to be much more vocal. There were moments when Jan and Rick seemed to be quite violently disagreeing, but Uncle Bob kept the team focussed on the key discussion points. There were several other areas that affected a couple of people round the table more than the others. Eventually, everyone seemed to have had their say – but still very little had been drawn on the plan and what had been looked like a bird's nest of lines and scribbles.

Uncle Bob said, "Right, think I can work with that now.

Dirk needs a walk and you lot deserve a coffee, so if Tim puts the kettle on and takes orders it will be ready for when you get back. I'll see you all in 30 minutes. Tim, I'll have my usual please as soon as the kettle boils."

Twenty-five minutes later we were back and Tim was just pouring the last coffee ready for us to take into the room. Jan had gone to sit in her car to keep warm and make a couple of calls but the walk gave me a chance to chat to a couple of other members of the team. Eric was keen to know what it was like to live in the city. He had only been there once in his life – "Too noisy and rushed for me."

When we returned there was a clean version of the boat drawing on the table with a mast and engine in situ. Uncle Bob then ran through his vision of how the boat would come together with some brief comments on dates, what needed to be done when and by whom. He then checked that everyone was OK with the plan. Mart asked a question about Easter. "Good point," said Uncle Bob and clarified a couple of points around that time on the plan.

"Normal Tuesday at 6.00 pm review meeting?" asked Jan looking at me.

"Fine with me," I replied.

"Unfortunately it won't be fine with you", said Uncle Bob. "We'll move it to Monday at 6.00 pm. You'll find the anti-natal classes in the village run at 6.00 pm on a Tuesday."

How did he know that? Villages! I had only found out a few days before that Karri was pregnant and I didn't remember mentioning it in the meeting. Jean knew. Maybe she had told him.

I stood corrected.

"We will start next Monday – have a good weekend." With that closing remark Uncle Bob left the room followed by Dirk, and the rest of us dispersed.

As I left, Uncle Bob said, "If you're happy with the plan, the team and the price I could do with the deposit we discussed before Monday. I have made it a rule over the years not to start a build without an agreed plan and a pile of cash!" He had a big grin on his face as he mocked the accountant in me ,but I knew there would be no boat without a deposit so the 'cash' was duly delivered the next morning.

6

DO IT AND DO IT NOW

Eric suggested I come down on Monday to see the start of the boat build. So it was that at 9.00 am I rolled up at the boat yard and went over to the big shed. Eric met me as I went in and called out, “Coffee for our guest, Tim!” as we meandered through the large open space that had been created in the middle of the shed.

“This is where we will build her.” There was a pride in Eric’s voice that made me pleased he was involved with the enterprise. He was clearly looking forward to building her.

I looked up and noticed all sorts of strange shapes and bits of wood, metal, carbon fibre and rope stored in the roof structure of the shed.

"What's that lot?" I asked.

"That's all the trial stuff that Uncle Bob has tried out over the years. Some were a great success and will be included in your boat. Some of them were not so good and honestly some of them were a bit of a disaster."

"What did the owners have to say about the disasters?"

"Oh he never tries out anything new on other people's boats – that's partly why he has *Meme*. He's always tweaking her and making changes that he hopes will make her better or faster. I think he should stop – she is the most perfect boat I know. But that's not his way."

Dirk came bounding over and I looked round to see Uncle Bob coming across the shed, clearly having a good look round at the newly cleared space.

"Tim has the kettle on. Do you want your normal?" Eric asked Uncle Bob.

"Sounds good to me – do you think you have enough space at the far end?"

"I have measured it and it's tight but OK."

"Let's take the mixing bench over to the other side and then you will be able to move around better."

Tim arrived with the coffee and we all sorted out milk and sugar. There was more chat about preparations and then Uncle Bob said, "Let's do it. Let's do it now."

Eric and Tim put down their coffee and started to move some large pieces of wood into the space. Uncle Bob moved to this growing pile of wood and took the sail bag off his shoulder. He pulled out a few sheets of paper. As the wood came in Uncle Bob would look carefully at each piece and then make a comment about it. Eric would mark the wood and Tim would bring in the next piece. It was fascinating to watch and before I knew it two hours had passed and I realised I needed to be at the office. The team were still working so I slipped out, I thought unnoticed, until I heard a shout of "Have a good day!" just before I closed the door of the shed.

They were still sorting wood when I returned at 5.00 pm. Tim looked exhausted and said, "I can't believe how hard these two work – it's no wonder they still race so hard."

I was thirsty and thought a pint in the pub on the way home would be a good idea. I had only been in a couple of times since the party and not at all since the boat build had started.

"I see you have started a boat, City Boy." The voice came from the group in the corner. "Going to win this year then?"

"Not sure she will be ready to win this year."

"What about you, boy? Are you ready to win?"

It was true. I hadn't sailed for some years and even then I wasn't great. I needed some help.

"Leave him alone Chris," came another voice from the table. "He's going to be a dad!" Graeme had come to my rescue.

"Does that mean the round is on him?"

"OK, drinks on me," I said and went over to join in the locals' banter at the table in the corner – I felt safe with Graeme there.

"Eric says he lived near the Prime Minister in the city. Is he as out of touch as he looks?" This was Chris trying to break the ice. I tried to think of a witty reply but failed and we fell back to talking about sailing.

And so it was that I quickly dropped into a pattern of popping in occasionally on the way home from the office both to the boat yard and the pub. It didn't seem to matter what time I dropped by the yard. There were always people working. There was a constant buzz of activity from the shed. The day always started with a coffee and chat with those who were in the shed. The chat was all about what had to be achieved that day and Uncle Bob would often run throughthe tasks for the next couple of days so that everyone knew what was going on and who was due in later in the week.

"Rick is in tomorrow so we need to finish the channel to the engine bay today. Tim, are you on top of the dowel plugs we will need? Don't forget, no surprises."

At 1.00 pm every day whoever was in the yard would stop and gather around a make shift table put up on trestles. The banter was rarely about work. Eric and Mart would chat away, asking Tim about his latest adventures with Janice and sharing the recent tales of village life. Mart seemed to have an ability to see the positive and humour in all the weird and wonderful situations that were discussed.

Then every Monday evening when the work stopped at 6.00 pm, the team would gather in the office to discuss the build with me. The meeting followed a very simple pattern with everyone in the room saying what had gone well that week, what was not going so well and what was happening next week. If someone was falling behind with work Mart, would often say, "I'll give you a hand with that tomorrow, we'll soon be back on track."

The issues that needed discussing by the whole team were led by Uncle Bob, but generally the team trusted the others to be getting on with what they had to do. I was pleased to be part of these discussions and surprised about how much Uncle Bob was prepared to let me hear things that the team were struggling with.

As the days started getting longer, the talk in the shed turned to this season's racing and it was noticeable that the boats in the yard outside were slowly returning one by one to the moorings in the bay. Mart was going to focus his mid week sailing season with Eric. Tim was going to do mid-week with Graeme and this left a space on Uncle Bob's boat for me to join the crew for the season.

"What's Karri doing on Wednesdays this year?" asked Uncle Bob.

"I don't think she has any plans 'til the baby is born," I replied.

Paul called that evening. "Are you out racing in your boat yet?"

"Not yet, but she's looking great and they're doing a brilliant job on her."

"Make sure they are sticking to the plan. If you don't keep pressing them this is when the timescales slip and the price goes up. Give them an inch and they'll take a mile."

"I think I am on it – when are you coming down?"

"Soon, mate. Soon."

7

EAT YOUR GREENS

It was a beautiful early spring evening. We had just finished tea when a knock came at the door. I gathered up my stuff, kissed Karri and went to the door to go off for the mid-week racing. At the door was Uncle Bob with Dirk.

"Dirk needs a walk", he said.

"Aren't we sailing?" I replied.

"Well I am, but I thought it was a perfect evening for Karri to join us and have a go at sailing. Is she free?"

Dirk looked at me with a knowing look that said – don't fight it, we can have a good walk.

Karri came to the door and after a brief chat about the

possible practical issues, all of which Uncle Bob seemed to have thought through, she agreed to go. Uncle Bob took my kit bag of sailing gear and held Karri by the arm; the bump, Karri and Uncle Bob moved down the steps to the road. Dirk looked up at me. I put my walking boots on and set off up the hill to the point where we could sit and watch the racing together.

As the race neared the end I saw Uncle Bob peel off and head back to the moorings. He had done this the previous couple of weeks with me but somehow I was concerned that things might not be right with Karri and the baby so I jogged down the hill with Dirk trotting beside me to the pub where I knew the sailors would gather once the boats were packed up. It was here that the serious work of eating, drinking and, most importantly, discussing the racing happened.

Karri was fine. In fact more than fine. She had a glow about her. Uncle Bob just said, "Great helm you've got there" and retired to the bench outside where I had first met him with Dirk.

"He let you helm *Meme*?" I was flabbergasted. I had only been allowed to trim the main sheet.

"Well I held the bit of wood and did what I was told to", said Karri grinning the smile that made me fall in love with her in the first place. "Why didn't you tell me how great sailing is?"

"I've been watching you boy, and you ain't no Graeme or even Eric. But this little lassie, well... is she your secret weapon boy? When you were shouting off about winning the trophy at prize giving we didn't know you had a secret weapon. Trouble is you have gone and spoilt your own plan – she'll calf down before the end of the season judging by the size of her!"

Well what do you say? Villages!

In the shed the next morning the pre-work chat still appeared to revolve around how natural Karri was at the helm. Mart seemed to pick up on my slightly crest-fallen look and changed the conversation to how well the boat was coming along.

"We've done a lot of the main planking and she is really starting to take shape. In a couple of days we can probably start plugging the holes – that's a boring job! Each one has to be done individually and getting it right makes all the difference to the look and performance. But boy oh boy it is dull. Every time we start it I think it's not too bad with the first one but after five I want to do something else and by the time we are up to 50 I don't want to see another plug in my life ever again! I call it eating my greens. Tim has been making the plugs haven't you Tim?"

"Oh, what? Yes."

"That's a boring job as well but we've all done it when we were the apprentice. I am sure it taught me something but not entirely sure what now."

Uncle Bob arrived. He started to say something and I caught Mart shaking his head out of the corner of my eye and Uncle Bob stopped and said, "Varnishing the interior parts today – how is everyone fixed for that? Tim – plugs coming on OK?"

There were general nods and a couple of questions about order of priority for varnishing and then I left to go to the office.

The day passed slowly for me. I had no client meetings that day and this meant I had no excuse not to get done all those tasks that Jean needed me to do. By 4.30 pm I had done all I could cope with so decided to walk home via the boat shed to see what progress had been made.

"Over here," I heard Mart call as I came into the shed. Mart, Eric, Tim and Uncle Bob were all varnishing small parts of wood that appeared to be hanging around all over one end of the shed.

"What is this?" I asked looking at a particularly strange shaped piece.

"Oh that is a support bar for under the cockpit." Uncle Bob didn't even look up from his careful work.

"Why are you varnishing that so well? No one will ever see it."

"*No,* that's true but *we* will know and you wanted to have a boat for more than a lifetime so we need to pay attention to the details," Uncle Bob replied. "Are you OK for sailing with me on Sunday?" I wanted to say "Don't you want to take Karri?" But that seemed petulant and so I said yes.

Sunday was a windy day. As we stood on the bouncing foredeck rigging the jib whilst still on the mooring, Uncle Bob started to chat to me about the conditions and the rig set-up. It was strange; I was starting to understand what made the difference between Uncle Bob and some of the others in the fleet. Every time he took *Meme* out he would set her up specifically for the conditions that day and if they changed during the race he would make adjustments.

"We are without Jamie today so you will be doing foredeck

duty if that's OK with you. It will be a wet one!" He ran through the basics of the foredeck work and showed me where everything was. "Don't rush it when we come to raise the spinnaker – it's much better to get it up right first time than to have to do it again or worse, to shred it!"

We went out and I had to say it was a very different view of the racing from the foredeck in a blow. Hand holds, rigging points and safety lines all take on much greater importance when you are bouncing around outside the relative shelter of the cockpit and relative simplicity of just trimming the mainsheet. It was a steep learning curve to be out there but we got round and I managed to do the tasks required of me. At the end of the race the crew were really complimentary and as we came ashore Tim came over to congratulate me.

"I never would have guessed you would be that good on the foredeck."

"I'll take that as a compliment," I replied. He went red as I laughed and Janice came over to his rescue.

I slept well that night and so didn't notice Karri getting up at 4.00 am.

8

THE WORLD WON'T END

Being at the hospital with Karri for the birth of our first child was the most fantastic day of my life. I had a spring in my step and just wanted to go round and tell everyone. I left the hospital at 3.00 pm to go home to get some bits and thought I would pop in on the team at the boat yard to let them know as I was passing. I knew something was up as soon as I went into the shed, but being so full of the birth I missed the signals. Dirk stayed in his bed in the corner of the shed keeping his head down, Eric barely nodded as I entered and Mart took me off to the office saying, "Come in here and have a coffee."

I told him the news – he was delighted but didn't call the others in.

"Where's Uncle Bob?" I asked.

"Must be in one of the other sheds," Mart replied. At that point I realised something was up. I had watched Uncle Bob and Eric work together – they both had strong opinions about the best way to do things. They both had a drive and energy that they put into everything they did, be it in the yard or on the water. However, they dealt with Tim very differently. Uncle Bob was quietly encouraging and didn't mind bending the rules a bit to help Tim along; Eric pushed Tim to do his best and made him stick to things. It was normally Eric's voice you could hear in the workshop giving instructions. This dynamic tension between Eric and Uncle Bob seemed to be the strength at the core of the yard and I was concerned that something must have happened between them.

"OK, what's happened?"

Mart then started talking in whispered tones. Apparently they had come to the point where the plugs were required to fill all the screw holes. Tim had been tasked with making these in his spare time through the build so far. They needed several hundred of these plugs and if he had done ten or so a day they would have had plenty by now. Unfortunately, he had only made about five in total and they weren't very good. Uncle Bob had taken him into the office for a chat. This had not lasted long and Tim had come out looking very sheepish and disappeared over to his bench. The day had been re-organised and Eric was now doing some work on the mast and Uncle Bob had gone off to the other shed.

At that moment there was a shout from the direction of Tim's bench. Mart looked out of the office door.

"I'd better go over and help," said Mart.

"I'll go back to the hospital," I replied.

Then the shed door opened and Uncle Bob came in. Dirk looked up and trotted over. He walked straight to Tim's bench.

"How many have you done?"

"Thirty-five useable." I could hardly hear Tim's reply.

"As I said earlier Tim, the world won't end. It will be hard work but we can fix this. You need to let Graeme know you won't be sailing tonight." Then turning to me he said, "Great news about Karri and the baby. I assume that means I am down a crew member for this evening?" How did he know so quickly?

Tim had disappeared outside to phone Graeme and I took the opportunity to ask Uncle Bob if everything was OK.

"Yes thanks. We had a slight problem this morning when Tim was unable to deliver what he had promised but we are on it now and should be back on track by the morning."

Tim came back into the shed. "All sorted," he mumbled.

"Let's have a look at what you've done so far", Uncle Bob replied.

They looked together through the box of plugs. Uncle Bob then said, "Eric, can you let my crew know *Meme* is not going out tonight when you see them. Give my love to Karri and tell her she can start sailing again as soon as she wants."

I left at this point to go and see Karri. The next time I was in the shed was Friday. Tim came up to me.

"Just because I am from outside the village don't think I don't know what is going on here," I said.

"But I –"

"No Tim, this is all about you lot from the sailing club doing all you can to fleece me of money for a boat that will take too long to build so I can't race it this year, won't be a good boat when I finally get it and therefore do all you can, however under-hand, to stop an outsider winning your precious trophy. Well, us city types know underhand and devious, we see it every day, and the problem is Tim, you are just not good enough at it to win."

By this point the shed was silent. Dirk had moved to Tim's side and was tucked under his legs.

"Sorry seems a bit small and futile now," said Tim and shuffled off.

Mart came over.

"Tim and Uncle Bob missed the mid-week racing last night. Tim let Graeme down as well. Uncle Bob and Tim worked until 2.00 in the morning to get the plugs done; I brought them some hot-pot from the pub at 9.30pm after the sailing was over and even Eric popped in for an hour on his way home from winning to make a few before Uncle Bob sent him home. We are back on track now."

"Oh."

Crestfallen, I went over to Tim to try and apologise.

Uncle Bob came in to the shed at that moment.

"Tim telling you how well we got on yesterday with the plugs he made?" Uncle Bob said as he headed off to the office, "Tim, bring us a cup of coffee each please." Then, looking over to me, he continued, "OK to join me for a quick chat?"

I followed Uncle Bob in to the office and we sat down.

"I have had a letter from your friend Paul asking me to build a boat for him."

"Yes – I was so pleased with what you were doing on mine I recommended you."

"But he lives in the city."

"Yes...?"

"And he wants it by Christmas."

"Yes. You have room in the other shed don't you?"

"That's true but I don't know him, Dirk doesn't know him and you know I am not really very good at building two boats at the same time. I wanted to let you know I will be saying no to Paul."

I must have looked puzzled.

"I appreciate your efforts to get me more work. Thank you. The thing is by the time you get to my age you have worked out what you are good at and what you are not so good at. Jan, she can make sails for ten, 15, maybe 20 boats at a time. She has a very ordered mind and uses that computer thing of hers to keep track of everything. When she is here she is 100 per cent on this boat and your sails, but when she goes back to her loft she will be working on a number at any one time. I don't work well like that. I can do repairs on one whilst we build another, but a build takes all my mind so I know I won't do a good job for Paul and your boat would suffer too. That's not good for me or my business."

I thought I understood but it still seemed strange to me. I was not sure I would ever understand villagers.

"Must go," I said. "I have got a new client meeting this morning – can I borrow Dirk?"

9

WHAT ARE YOU GOING TO DO DIFFERENTLY?

Karri had come home over the weekend and her parents had come down to help out for the first few weeks so she was adamant that I went along to the Monday meeting at the boat yard, as usual, the week after the birth. I arrived in good time and could see the hull looking in really good shape and the decking starting to come together. Mart was sweeping up the wood chips from the day's work as always. In fact, it was only varnishing day that I hadn't seen him sweeping. Eric walked next to me as we made our way to the office and asked if I had thought about having the baby christened. I arranged for him to come and chat with me and Karri later in the week and sat down to join the others in the room. All except Rick were there. Just as Uncle Bob was about to start we heard the shed door shut and knew Rick was on his way in.

"Slight change of plan for the meeting tonight everyone." Uncle Bob opened up the meeting and went on, "We are thrilled that we are now building a boat for three rather than just Karri and the accountant, so Eric's wife has made one of her famous chocolate cakes and Tim has made 'real coffee', whatever that may be, so let's have a cheer for all of them and a little speech from the proud Dad as we eat cake."

I was caught a bit on the hop. I didn't really know what to say. We shared cake and some very nice coffee and even Jan seemed to relax a little and join in the banter around the table as I thought about what I might say.

"I'm really pleased to be a Dad. I sometimes feel I've fathered two children and the boat seems to have taken more time so far than my son, Luke. I have learnt some lessons though and who knows, they might even come in handy as I do more as a father."

There was a cheer at this point and I realised that I wasn't expected to say much more – which was a relief.

Uncle Bob then brought everyone to order saying, "Yes, I think the Africans have a proverb about it taking a whole village to bring up a child so I suppose we all have our part to play. Now I am sure we're on track with most things, so I would like Tim to tell us a little bit about what he has been up to in the last few weeks." I was surprised by this, given the experience of the previous week, but it didn't seem to surprise anyone else – least of all Tim.

As everyone in the room turned to look at Tim he straightened up and started to describe the work he'd been doing. He focussed on a new sheeting system that he'd been working on with Jan and Mart that would make the boat easier for Karri to work with. He went into the reasons why they had looked into it, what benefits it would bring and the changes to the agreed design that it would require. It seemed that Tim was leading this development. Jan nodded when Tim referred to her input into the process of changing the design and it seemed as though everyone was happy with the changes.

Tim also mentioned the plugs, apologising to all and explaining what he had learnt from the experience and what he was going to do differently in the future to ensure that he didn't put everyone in that position again.

When the meeting was over I asked if I could walk to the pub with Uncle Bob so I could have a chat. I was bothered that Mart was the rigger but it was Tim making the changes. Uncle Bob answered my concern by saying, "When asked if Ringo Starr was the best drummer in the world John Lennon is rumoured to have replied 'He is not even the best drummer in the Beatles.'" He carried on as I was still looking confused, "A team is made of people who bring a range of skills to that team. Some of those are specific skills for the project, like Jan with the sails. Others are just good to have around and they do things that some people don't notice or value – that's Mart. We wouldn't be on track on this build without him. He is a good rigger.

Don't worry, he's happy to let Tim have a moment of glory on the sheeting, I've talked to him about it."

At the pub Chris was there to meet us. "Evening! As it is not you winning, who is your money on for the mid-week trophy? Eric says you've got a new sheeting system on the boat – how's that going to work then? Have you tried it on *Meme* or is the City Boy trying this on his own? Have you even helmed a boat in the racing yet, City Boy? How is the secret weapon coming on? He lived near the Prime Minister you know." Uncle Bob and Dirk seemed to have slipped into the pub and got a pint and were seated at their usual bench before Chris had finished, leaving me to fend off his enquiries.

As the nights started to close in, the mid-week racing was starting to get intense, with Graeme and Eric fighting it out for the trophy. I was starting to feel more confident around the boat and even occasionally starting to make the required adjustments before being asked to do so by Uncle Bob. *Meme* was not only a very beautiful boat she was also a pleasure to sail. Everything about her just worked and she was quick, very quick.

The final mid-week race came. As we stood on the foredeck sorting out the sails and the rest of the crew were coming aboard, Uncle Bob turned to me and said, "Would you like to helm tonight?"

I should have been delighted – I had waited all summer for this moment and six months ago would have said yes immediately, but now... well now I knew what it took to sail her, now I knew how much Uncle Bob loved her and what she represented, and now I was only weeks away from having my own boat. I was scared. I was scared that I might not sail her well. I was scared I might break something but most of all I was scared that if I helmed *Meme* then my own boat would be a disappointment.

"It'll be OK – I am staying on board," Uncle Bob said reassuringly, seeing my uncertainty.

"I'd be delighted," I said and went back towards the cockpit to start preparing.

"Come back – you're not finished here," I heard from the foredeck. Seemed being helmsman didn't necessarily make you captain!

Well, we were close to the start line when the gun went but probably not as close as we could have been. With some help I picked the shifts up the first beat and we rounded the first mark in second place. We stayed well in the hunt for the lead so that coming down the last leg we were battling it out with Graeme for first with Eric just behind. I was concentrating so hard I didn't hear what Uncle Bob said the first time so the shout of "Peel off!" came as quite a surprise and I caught the crew out by throwing over the helm and swinging all the way round to sit still facing the wind. Once everyone had collected themselves we had a bit of a laugh about my smooth helming and then headed back to the mooring, making sure we avoided crossing the line.

As we packed the boat away I finally plucked up the courage to ask Uncle Bob why he never crossed the line in the racing.

"It doesn't seem right to me to take people's money to build boats for them to win a race and then race against them myself. Seems as though they could accuse me of not making their boat as fast as mine and then they wouldn't trust me and everything would be so much harder."

"But you're leading nearly every race when you peel off – don't you want the prize?"

"The trophy would be nice, but that's not what success looks like for me. Just because you can do something doesn't mean you should or you must do it."

With that he went back to flaking the jib and I was left thinking about what I would choose to do.

10

THE BAG OF ANSWERS

The end was getting close. My boat looked very nearly finished and it seemed the whole team was now around nearly all the time with the exception of Jan, but even she came most days to check things out and provide information. Sometimes she would get something that looked like a sail out of the car and give it to Mart.

I arrived early for the Monday meeting and decided now was the time to chat to Eric about the bag that Uncle Bob seemed to carry all the time.

"Ah, that's what Uncle Bob calls his 'bag of answers'," said Eric. I looked puzzled and he went on, "In there is everything he needs to keep to hand to do with this boat. He has four main sections: the people involved with all their contact information, roles, etc.; the plans and build information; the list of what success looks like – he ticks them off when we achieve them; and then all the documents that come with bits of the boat, invoices, manuals, certificates, etc."

"So what happens to all of that?"

"Follow me."

We went through a small door in the side of the main shed and I found myself in a long room with pegs on the wall. Each peg had a canvass bag on it with a small wooden plaque above it and on each plaque was engraved a name.

"This," said Eric "is where we come when we need to know something about any of the boats that come back here for repair."

"Wow!" I said, genuinely impressed. I thought I was the only person in the village with any kind of system and record keeping – it certainly seemed like that when I did their accounts, but here was everything we needed to know. I could see Eric's boat name on a peg and *Meme* at the far end, and some I didn't recognise.

"There are more here than I see out racing."

"We don't just build for this village or just sailing boats you know. That one is Bill's fishing boat, that one is raced at Cowes and that one is on a Loch in the north somewhere, we don't see that one back often!"

Eric then glanced down at his watch. Time for the meeting.

The meeting followed the standard pattern but I noticed this time that Eric was much more vocal. He was very keen to ensure that all the little jobs were being picked up and completed and he had started to write a list. He was putting names and completion times against each job and when the meeting was over he pinned this to the office door. The list had some items on it with no name or time. "What happens about these?" I asked.

"We all chip in to make sure the boat gets finished on time but as it is my list, if no one else does it I will make sure it gets done."

"Are you free if we get her in the water next Wednesday lunchtime?" Uncle Bob was looking at me but also Eric.

"Will she be ready to sail then?" I asked.

"No, but we need to get the hull in the water to finish off a few bits and pieces and it helps some of the team to have a deadline to focus on." Uncle Bob smiled at Eric and he smiled back – I think I knew who they meant.

"We'll all come down for the show," said Chris as I popped into the pub for a pint on my way home. "Is the secret weapon going to name her?" A name. I hadn't really thought about that. My mind was in a panic and it was clear that Chris could see that finally he had hit a nerve with all his questions. He started to reel off names like a naming machine gun and with each he made me less and less secure about any that were popping into my head.

Graeme came over just in time to rescue me and said "You don't need to decide – ask someone close to you who's got that skill. You do numbers not words – someone you know must do words." He was right. I did do numbers. I knew the build was on budget; I had worked with Uncle Bob on that right from the start. I knew what positions Eric and

Graeme needed in the final race to ensure victory in the series. Words though, they were different – people had feelings about words and this meant it mattered what we called the boat.

11

BEER OR CHAMPAGNE?

Wednesday came and I told Jean I wouldn't be in all day. I was too excited about the whole thing to concentrate on work. Dad had come down to see the launch but for now was staying up at the house to help Karri with the baby. I was down at the yard early expecting to be the first one in and enjoy a bit of early autumnal quiet.

However, when I arrived the boat was still in the shed and the lights were on. I went in and heard someone say "Nearly there!" It was Rick working on the electrics.

"I thought we were launching today," I said.

"Oh we are – won't be a problem. Can you see a red port

side light on?"

"No."

"Now?"

"Yes."

"Brilliant!"

There was a bit of banging and what sounded like the collecting of tools and a very dishevelled Rick came out from the cabin and started climbing down the ladder.

At that moment Mart came out of the kitchen area with three cups of coffee and met Rick at the bottom of the ladder.

"Brilliant!" said Rick again. "Perfect timing! She's all yours."

I sat down at the coffee bench and Mart joined me.

"Rick looks awful. Has he been here all night?" I asked Mart.

"Yup", said Mart.

"What happened?"

Mart then told me the tale of the previous 24 hours. He started by saying that they all knew Rick and that he was always a man who liked to work to a deadline and was normally the last to finish the work on a boat but this had been worse than normal. Apparently, he had arrived to finish the work just after lunch. He had fitted several bits when he realised that one of the parts he had with him was not working. He had rung round and found that there was one available at a yard about two hours' drive away. He was about to leave to get this when Mart had offered to do that so that he could carry on and fit the rest of the bits. Mart had taken Rick's van to the other yard to pick up the part and then driven back. Then it seemed that some of the installation was more of a challenge than had been expected, so when Mart brought Rick some food from the pub to keep him going he'd been asked for a bit of help to check things through and had ended up staying the night working with Rick to get it all done.

Mart had just finished the story when Uncle Bob arrived with Dirk and asked if the boat was ready to move to the yard ahead of launching. Mart said, in a very matter of fact way, that she was and Uncle Bob went outside to bring in the crane.

"I've brought a bottle of champagne", I said to Eric when he arrived.

"You'd better chat to Uncle Bob about that."

Once the boat was in the cradle and out in the yard I made a coffee for myself and Uncle Bob and asked him about the launch.

"You can splash champagne if you want to – is that a city thing?" he said in response to my showing him the bottle. "But I think you said success was winning the trophy – why don't you save the champagne for that?"

"Good point," I said. "but I still want to celebrate. What do you suggest?"

"The pub does a nice pint – I think this boat needs some beer in her life!"

I wandered over to the pub as the rest of the team gathered to make sure that everything was ready to get her in the water. As I returned, Dad and Karri came down the hill with the pushchair and Jan arrived in a car full of sail bags.

"Do you want to say anything before we put her in the

water?" Uncle Bob asked.

"Of course you do, City Boy," said Chris. "Tell us about the Prime Minister and the secret weapon!" Dad looked very confused. "I'll explain later," I said.

I started speaking to the small gathering.

"I have really enjoyed being part of the team who built this boat. You have all played your part and have been a great team to work with. For Karri and I the really hard work starts from now as Uncle Bob reminded me this morning – we built this boat to win a trophy, not just to have a boat. So I look forward to beating all of you out on the water!" There was a small cheer and a laugh from Tim. "I would like to name this boat *Ziggadive* – it is the name my sister gave my first boat when she was four and I promised her I would call every boat I owned that and so – *Ziggadive,* may God bless all who sail in her." And with that I threw my pint of beer over the bows.

"Amen!" shouted Eric, and Uncle Bob allowed the cradle to roll gently down the slipway.

She floated elegantly on the high tide and Mart started the engine and moved her round to the dock side where the team then gathered to step the mast with the crane.

"Good name," whispered Chris as he brushed passed me on the way back to the pub.

There was a flurry of activity and Uncle Bob suggested I took the family to the pub whilst they got on and prepared her for me to go aboard.

A couple of hours later we were all on board looking round below deck as Tim, Jan and Mart worked on deck with the rig and sails.

"If the weather is good we might be OK for a sail tomorrow, but I think looking at those clouds it would be better on Friday," said Uncle Bob.

I was really pleased with all that I saw and couldn't wait to get on and have a go.

Thursday morning came and the wind was blowing very hard. *Ziggadive* had joined the other boats at the moorings in the harbour and I could see the yard tug boat moored behind her and the occasional head stick up though the hatchway. Dirk strolled up and sheltering from the wind, sat by my leg and the Uncle Bob joined me.

"Best to leave Tim to it today I think," he said. "We have a couple of things we want to test and the weather will be much better for you tomorrow. Would you like me to get Eric's wife to look after Junior so Karri can come out with you on the maiden sail?"

"No thanks, it's OK. Mum has come down as well and she really doesn't like boats so she will happily have Luke."

"See you tomorrow."

Friday was just perfect. Uncle Bob took us out to the boat, Tim came as crew and to show us all how to use the new sheeting system. *Ziggadive* handled like *Meme*. She cut through the waves easily and quickly and although there were no other boats to compare against I knew she would be quick.

We worked our way through the list of requirements Dad had given me a while back and realised that all that we had included in the Essential, Important and Nice to have categories were there. We tried all points of sailing and as we went along Uncle Bob wandered the deck checking things, chatting to Tim, adjusting bits and making the odd note. Karri helmed and it was great to see how much she had learnt over the summer and just how much she was enjoying *Ziggadive*.

"She's perfect," I said.

"Well nearly," replied Uncle Bob. "Tim will do some tweaks over the next couple of days."

Eric, Uncle Bob, Tim and Mart all joined me on Sunday for the first race of *Ziggadive*'s career and although we were well down the fleet we had a great time and knew that ultimately she would be a contender.

12

CHOOSING MY TEAM

Christenings are strange things. The family came and so did a number of friends from the city. We had a house full and had to suggest to a few that they stay at the pub, while a couple of others stayed with Eric and his wife. It was the vicar who spurred me into action that day. His sermon was drifting around me when he made a throwaway comment that it would be a few years before the new baby would be crew material.

Crew – I needed to sort a crew for next season. I had made the assumption that Tim would be there but I hadn't asked and if he sailed with Graeme he was much more likely to win... I really needed a core group of four of us and then a second group of people to join when required.

As we walked back from the church to the house I mentioned my thinking to Karri. After her initial disappointment that I hadn't been giving the vicar (or Luke for that matter) my full attention, she suggested that the christening party would be a good time to sound a few people out and that she had a few ideas as well.

If Tim was up for it we had someone who knew the tides locally and the boat, but what we lacked was a bit of flare and fun. It was at this point in the party that I realised what quiet people we were. I moved round the room hoping to find someone who would bring the zest for life to our team that I felt we needed. Failing to find anyone who wasn't already in deep conversation, I decided to step outside. There was Uncle Bob with Dirk sat on our garden bench looking out over the sea and sampling a glass of the beer I had bought in from the local brewery for the party.

"How's the crew selection coming on?" I decided to ignore the 'How did he know?' voice in my head and replied, "Not great actually, we need a bit of life on the team and I'm struggling to find someone."

This seemed to surprise Uncle Bob and he sat up with a more intense look on his face.

"Interesting – tell me more about the person you're looking for."

"Well I want someone to add a bit of a laugh and a joke to our sailing, someone who will lighten the mood when we have a bad race, someone who is willing to have a go at something different."

"Do any of your clients fit the description? It may help me to think of the right person to suggest."

"I suppose it's a cross between Jimmy who runs the pub and Sarah who runs the B&B up at the farm."

"Well why don't you ask them if they know of anyone? Jimmy is not here but I assume Sarah is."

This seemed like a good idea. I knew that Jimmy wouldn't sail with me – he couldn't give up the time from the pub and Sarah didn't sail – she had told me that on our first meeting when I came up to the farm to do the accounts for the B&B. Sarah was what most of my friends in the city thought of when you said farmer's wife. Strong, hearty with a great sense of humour, little fazed her and she never seemed to sit down and do nothing. Friends who stayed at the B&B wondered when she slept and loved the breakfast. In fact Paul preferred to stay at Sarah's B&B than with us mainly due to the breakfast.

I wandered back into the party and found Sarah. She was with a small group of people I didn't recognise. I said hello and she introduced me to her husband, two sons and a friend of the sons from the next village. We exchanged pleasantries and then I asked about crew. Sarah immediately said, "You know my feelings about boats – no chance."

However, her younger son seemed queit interested and the friend said his Dad was looking for someone to sail with. As I chatted to the family it became obvious that Rory took after his mother and was really quite a laugh. He was also a big strong lad who would be a real asset on the crew. However, I had learnt a bit from Uncle Bob so

I suggested, "Why don't we go for a walk tomorrow and chat about this some more?" He looked a little surprised but agreed and then suggested asking Derek (his friend's Dad) as well.

After a short walk the following day – it was too cold to be out for long – and a long drink in the pub, it was agreed that Rory and Derek would join us for a few practice sails over the winter to see if we could all work together for the race season.

13

PRACTICE, PRACTICE AND MORE PRACTICE

Two weeks after the christening on a chilly late autumn morning the five of us gathered on the harbour wall to have our first try with *Ziggadive* as a crew. I was there first. Karri had been up early to feed the baby and I couldn't get back to sleep. A bacon sandwich and a coffee later, I was hurrying down the hill to meet the others.

I had chatted to Jan about the rig and she had written up some notes which I had in my bag. I wasn't sure that I really understood them so I was hoping that Hannah (a friend of Tim's) who worked with Jan might be able to help out.

Derek arrived with cakes, a captain's hat for me and some spare gear for Rory. We decided to go to the pub for a coffee first just to work out our plan for the day. Tim took charge of the planning whilst I bought coffee – it was good to hear laughter coming from the table already but I did wonder how long it would be before Tim decided we had to focus on the practice.

When I got back to the table Rory moved round so that I could sit between him and Hannah. Tim summarised what they had agreed so far and laid out what he felt would be a good result from the day.

"That sounds like a great day," said Hannah enthusiastically and we all agreed, if not quite so positively.

We took the yard day boat out to Ziggadive. She was one of the few boats now left in the water; most were on the hard standing by the yard. Tim helped Hannah aboard and they set to work getting the sails sorted whilst I got to know Derek and Rory and explained how the cockpit work was going to be divided up.

"Ready to hoist the sails, Skipper?" Tim called. Wow, 'Skipper'! That sounded good but inside I felt a bit of a fraud. It was really at this moment that I realised what Uncle Bob had said about beer and champagne – building the boat was the easy part – learning to sail it well enough to win the trophy, well, that was a whole other ball game and not one that my city money could buy. I was in charge now. It was a good job Tim was there because at that moment going back to the pub and just day sailing *Ziggadive* on picnics looked like a really good result.

"Let's go! We've got a trophy to win," someone shouted from the foredeck.

"Hoist sails!" I shouted back and we got on with the day.

This was the first of many similar days through the winter. They were cold and sometime miserable days. The routine of practice was difficult at times but we grew closer together as we learnt what each of us was capable of. We played games, we swopped roles and we tested ourselves against Uncle Bob and a couple of his friends in the very early spring as soon as Uncle Bob had *Meme* back in the water.

The time came to work out who was going to be in the team for the summer.

This was a job for the kitchen table – so one evening I invited Tim round for dinner and afterwards the three of us sat round the table to work out the crew.

It was Karri who asked the question.

"Tim, what does Janice think about Hannah being on the crew?"

"Oh she's fine."

"Are you sure?"

"Well we do have the odd silent night in the pub on a Saturday when I have been out practising – I thought it was because I hadn't taken her into town to shop, but now you mention it..."

We could both see his mind working and re-thinking the last few months in the light of this new information.

"But Hannah's just a mate – she's a good sailor as well – we need her on the boat."

Karri sat for a moment and then replied.

"It would be nice to have her – and yes she is a good sailor, but we need you more and we need a happy you more, and you're happy when things are good with you and Janice."

Tim looked a little puzzled – I was a little puzzled. We both looked at Karri and it just seemed right that Hannah wouldn't join our crew for the coming year. So it was that what I thought would take all evening ended up being a very quick decision and the team fell into place.

The following weekend I got a big hug from Janice and a thank you whispered in my ear – not sure that these two things were linked with the crew decision, but Tim looked like Dirk when you got his lead out.

14

ONE YEAR ON

It would be great to say that we won the trophy that first year but we didn't. It was close. Tim was a stalwart crew member throughout the season and Mart did a few evenings to cover when we were short. However, Eric and Graeme were both very good sailors and had the local knowledge to catch those shifts and tide changes.

We did do better when Karri was able to come down to helm but we weren't always able to get a babysitter. Tim was really good at making sure we stuck to the patterns that Uncle Bob had taught us both the year before. We followed the rigging guide from Jan and made adjustments as laid out during the initial trials.

In the summer Paul came down for a couple of weekends and my sister visited with her family for a holiday. We were able to use *Ziggadive* to go to the beaches in the next bay and have some picnics. She responded well to new helms and there were no big surprises as we went through the season.

Towards the end of the mid-week series Uncle Bob joined us one evening. He did main sheet for me as I had done for him the previous season. At the end of the season he came to me and congratulated me on a good season and said that if I was to bring the boat in early he would do some tweaks for me that would improve the speed and give me a better chance next year. I think he was being very gracious. Rumour had it that the night I couldn't make it to the racing *Ziggadive* had won the race by miles although Tim did try to lessen the blow by insisting there had been a very big and 'lucky' wind shift.

Ziggadive is in the yard at the moment and I've gone down to visit her a couple of times and meet with the team. It feels as though I'm home and she's never left.

Next year, what success looks like will not be just a dream; it will be a reality.

TRUST

The glue that holds a team together.

TRUST

The problem with trust is that it is invisible glue that holds the team together. If it was brightly coloured glue and we could all see it, life would be easy. We would know who we could trust and who trusted us. The challenge, particularly for newly formed teams, is that trust is not easily seen. It takes time to earn, build and maintain. It is often much easier to spot the signs of lack of trust. Fear is present when someone doesn't trust another individual or a selection of people within the team. Fear manifests itself in many ways, but within teams we see it as defensive behaviours and lack of willingness to engage and change.

When we don't trust ourselves, that can be just as challenging. We learn to adapt to the situation if we trust those around us. However, when we trust ourselves but not the others around us, we look to define what those others do and this leads to conflict and further mis-trust.

It is only when we build lasting, trusting relationships within a team that we can shape the team and the environment it works within, into something that is robust, flexible and ultimately successful.

For trust to work, all in the team will have to let go and be vulnerable in some situations. There are a few simple things that help to build trust, such as ensuring there are clearly defined roles and goals. However, if these are implemented in a draconian way, without care, listening and understanding of the individual skills and capacities, even this improved clarity will break the small amount of trust built and make the situation worse.

You can build trust in 2 ways - they often run in parallel

1. Ensuring close relationships where there is the opportunity to develop rapport, empathy and friendship

2. Factual knowledge built up through experience of the other person's performance and evidence of competence

Both are easily damaged and part of the role of the best leaders is mitigation of the damage done when trust between team members is broken. Swift action and providing the right environment for a journey of reconciliation are key skills that every effective long term team leader learns and develops.

4 TRAITS THAT MAKE A PROJECT TEAM SUCCESSFUL

ENERGY

Energy can be converted in form, but not created or destroyed

ENERGY

The simple rules of physics can be very frustrating to those of us who prefer to believe in a more artistic world of shades, subtle variance and creativity. Energy is one of those things that physics does rather well and it is true that if your team is to put energy into creating and completing tasks and projects they must get energy from somewhere.

Finding a good energy source for your team is not an easy task and different individuals within your team will recharge their own batteries in different ways. Some will require lots of interaction with others, some will look for new and exciting challenges, some will want to tick things off a list, whilst others will like to strive for hours in the solitary pursuit of perfection. All have a role within the balanced team at different times.

There are also things that sap the energy from a team. Like a poorly insulated home in the depths of winter, you can watch the energy and warmth drain from a team, particularly when members of the team do not take personal responsibility for the role and tasks they have to complete and deliver. Responsibility is different from accountability. When team members all feel and carry responsibility for the success of the team, there is an energy and drive about them. If we could harness it, we wouldn't need to build another power station ever again.

Success is another source of energy. We have all seen the victor in a race able to jog round for a lap of honour whilst the losers collapse on the track unable to stand any longer. Celebrate success, find the interim goals that break the project or task into points where the team has the opportunity to see a win and celebrate. The long, grinding pressure of endless, thank-less delivery will result in a de-motivated team lacking the energy for success.

As a leader, look out for those that are flagging and give them the opportunity to re-energise. More than once I have sent someone home for the afternoon and reaped the rewards the next day. My father has a saying - "The farmer had just got his cow to live on nothing when it died" - keep feeding the cows in your team!

NOTES

REACH

What can we get our arms round?

REACH

The leader of the most successful teams is the one that ensures that the team believes they can achieve the goal, tasks or vision laid out by the leader. Sometimes this is about blind trust in a very charismatic leader, at other times it is because the team is building on previous success, and sometimes it is just about ambition. Always, there must be a core belief that what is being asked of the team is possible.

Does the team know what success looks like? If they don't, how do they know if they can do it? Clear goal setting is key. There is also a role for matching the capacity of the team to the tasks and capabilities that will be required for success. It takes time to build a successful team. Yes one can buy in talent and capability, but the trust and energy required for long term success comes from time and energy being fed into the team in the correct way and with the correct timing.

It is just as important to stretch the team a little as it is to not over stretch the team. Tension is vital. When making rope, it is the tension in the process and the eventual product that provides the strength and resilience. Without some tension in the team, it will have no resilience. Too much and it will break, too little and it will flop about and not respond to the direction the leader wishes to go.

Building tension is about defining the reach of the team well and matching the roles, goals and successes to the capability and capacity of the team. Monitoring the tension and reach constantly within the team will ensure that the team don't snap or unravel.

NOTES

SUPPORT

You don't build a team - you support people and they build a team.

SUPPORT

Support has 3 contexts:

1. The support that is provided within the team
2. The support for the product or service of the team
3. The support the team members receive from outside the team

A team leader may be in control of some of this, but rarely are they able to control it all. The support the team receive for what they do feeds into the energy they have to complete tasks. Sometimes it is as simple as a "thank you", but better still is to know that what you produce is useful, usable and valued by those who receive it. If not, it will not be long before at least one team member starts to question why they are doing the tasks they have in front of them.

Creating the environment where support is given within the team is a key activity for the successful team leader. We are not all at our best every day or in every task. Sometimes we just need some support to get that thing done. When the team takes responsibility for the team success you see people looking to help those around them to do the best they can.

You will often see people within a team who get support in only two of the contexts described. Two can be OK. Obviously all three is ideal, but two is OK. However, if they get no support or only one of the three, that individual, and ultimately the team, will struggle to succeed.

Ensuring the team has that support and can see it through clear communication, strong connections with stakeholders and development of individuals will make for a successful team.

Without support, however clear the leader is about the reach and however much energy the team try to put in, ultimately it will all just crash down in an exhausted heap.

Support can be encouraged by sharing a clear vision and purpose, by consistent delivery of valuable outputs and by a culture of responsibility and holding each other to account. As with Trust, Energy and Reach, Support is easily lost. Given time and clear direction, this part of leading a team has the potential to become self sustaining.

NOTES

MARK

Mark Jarvis has 30 years of experience in bringing together teams for projects. By his own admission, some of these have been more successful than others, but each experience has helped to hone his understanding of the topic of the book. For nine years he worked at Fujifilm in the UK building teams in sales support and sales as part of a significant time of growth for the company. Since leaving Fujifilm he has established Hunmoco Ltd as a boutique consultancy facilitating the development of teams within a wide range of industries – automotive, communications, manufacturing, sport and charity.

CHRIS

Chris Powell is a Group Analyst and senior member of the Institute of Group Analysis. Having worked in commercial, charitable and public sector settings over the last 30 years, he now divides his time between clinical and organisational work where he brings together his experience as a clinician and senior analysis to help people understand what happens in groups and teams, how things go wrong, and how change can occur. Current clients include the Ministry of Justice, NHS, University of Leeds, Institute of Group Analysis, and Group Analysis North,

NOTES

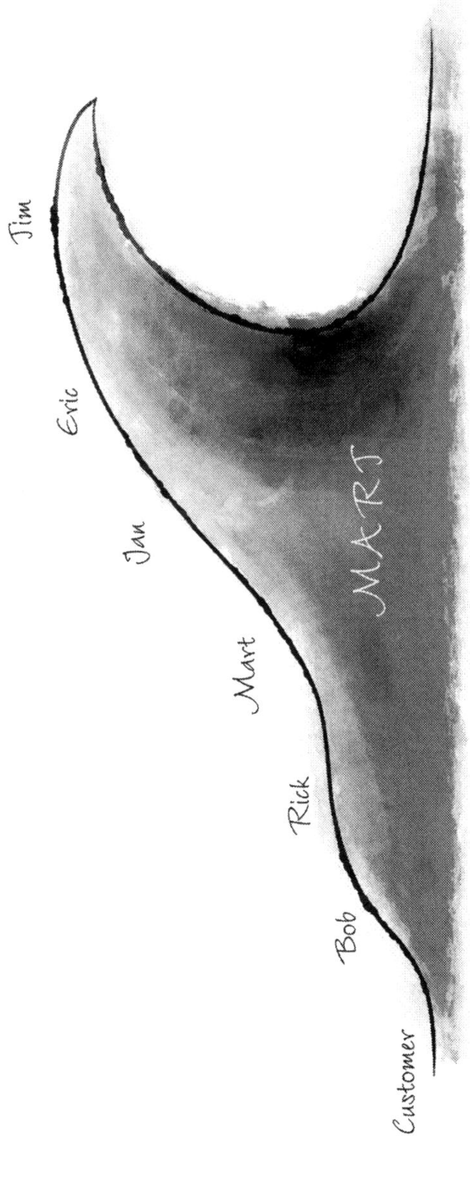

UNCLE BOB TEAM

UNCLE BOB BUILDS A BOAT

NOTES

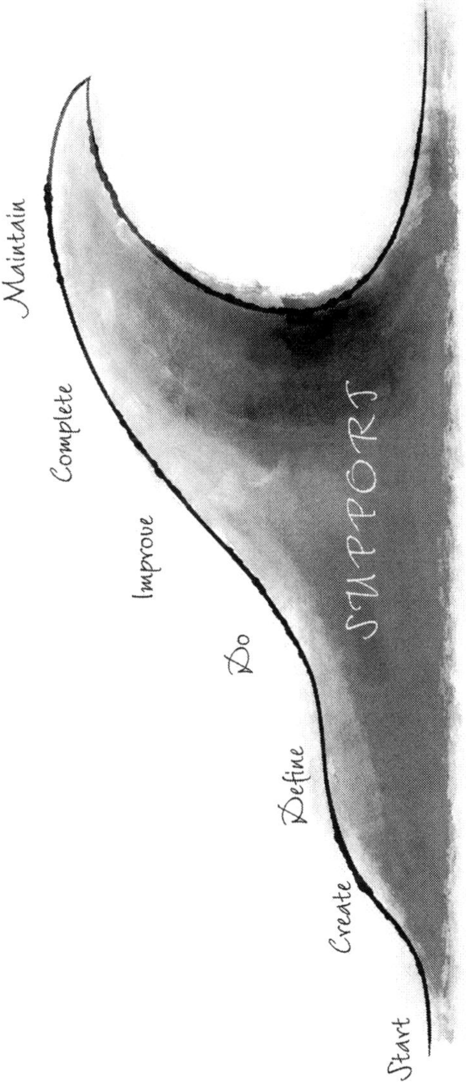

UNCLE BOB WORDS

UNCLE BOB BUILDS A BOAT

23193023R00062

Printed in Great Britain
by Amazon